# Getting Unstuck:

## *How Create The Life You've Always Wanted To Live*

By: Shawnda Patterson

# DEDICATION

To my mother, husband, and daughters. Mom, you encouraged me to follow my purpose wherever it may lead me. I didn't it know it at the time but that advice would change my life. To my incredibly amazing husband you knew I was a writer long before I did. Thank you for not allowing me to make excuses but to pursue my dreams with relentless tenacity. And, to my daughters Yanna, Kaya and Bria each of you have a special place in my heart. Sistars Rock!

"There is one quality that one must possess to win, and that is definiteness of purpose, the knowledge of what one wants, and a burning desire to possess it."

~ Napoleon Hill ~

# INTRODUCTION

A child's future is dreamy, filled with great desires which he might have no idea on how to fulfill. Still, dreaming is the gift of childhood. When you were a child you were very optimistic about your future. Maybe your own dreams involved becoming a doctor, lawyer or even a princess. It seemed like a joke, like only a few hours had passed by, then you blinked, and twenty years had gone by. Apparently, being a princess isn't a real thing so, you finally had to grow up and become an adult. And just like that, the childlike dreamer in you slowly began to die. Yeah, since those of your dreams didn't come true, what gives the assurance that any other dreams would come to pass? You didn't even make a conscious decision to give up, it just happened, and of course, it didn't happen at once- little by little before you got to the point where you are confused about your life. You may be wondering to yourself, "How in the world did I get here?" Maybe you expected to be married with children by now or be running your own multi-million dollar company but nope, that definitely didn't happen. Instead, your life might have gone like this: you married your high school sweetheart and you just knew you two would be together forever. Yet, here you are; divorced by the age of 30, twenty pounds overweight and working a job that you absolutely hate. The people closest to you don't even realize that you're just going through the motions. Truthfully, you haven't been genuinely happy in a long time. Somewhere along the line, things got off track and now you are desperate to be the version of yourself you've always desired to be. This book was written to help you resurrect the dreamer within you and show you that you don't have to live a limited life that doesn't make you fulfilled. In this book, you'll discover among other things: creating a vision, finding your purpose, the secret to happiness, how to resurrect an old dream and more. Yes, you can recreate the version of you that you thought was dead. It begins now.

# TABLE OF CONTENTS

INTRODUCTION ............................................. 6

CHAPTER 1 *Believing Is Seeing* ..................... 12

CHAPTER 2 *Finding Your Purpose* ................ 31

CHAPTER 3 *Watch Your Mouth* ................... 46

CHAPTER 4 *The Beauty Of Failures* .............. 54

CHAPTER 5 *Toxic Relationships* ................... 71

CHAPTER 6 *The Secret To Making Better Decisions* ....................................................... 85

CONCLUSION .............................................. 94

# CHAPTER 1
## *Believing Is Seeing*

Create a vision. How many times have you heard that before? You may already have your own vision board or even attended one of those new popular vision board parties. You cut out pictures of handsome men or women, mansions, exotic vacation destinations and of course, piles and piles of money. But, despite your incredibly creative and artsy project, it didn't work. There is so much more to creating a vision than simply cutting and pasting pictures on a board. Before you immediately dismiss the idea of visualization and categorize it as "new age nonsense", understand that there is scientific evidence which has proven the effectiveness of visualization techniques.

Let's first discuss the science behind visualization and then we'll make it practical. It all starts from the retina, where the brain initially processes visual stimulus. Next, it's the thalamus. Then the visual cortex. And lastly, the association cortex. Your brain attempts to filter these thoughts in terms of which ones are necessary and which ones are unnecessary. However, the longer you hold a vivid mental picture of something in your mind and metaphorically stamp that idea folder with the word "important", the harder it becomes for your brain to differentiate between what is imagined and what is real. To put it in laymen terms, visualization actually fools the brain into believing that the event you have imagined has already happened.

The implication of this is that you have to change your perception of yourself if you want to see changes in your life, and for you to move from where you are to where you want to be. Maslow called this theory self-actualization.

Originally, this term was coined by Kurt Goldstein as the possession of a desire to attain one's highest potential, via creativity and became popularized when Maslow incorporated it into his hierarchy of needs. According to Maslow, before a human would go on a quest for self-actualization, it must mean that his or her primary needs have been met- that of food, shelter, security and a sense of belonging. However, if someone has to focus on these primary needs all of his/her life, it becomes almost impossible for there to be self-actualization and thus, the person might never be happy. Maslow describes the good life as one directed towards self actualization, the pinnacle need. Below you will find some interesting characteristics of self-actualizers according to Maslow. Do you possess these characteristics?

- Efficient perceptions of reality: with self-actualizers, it isn't difficult at all to see through a façade, and know when something is real or when it isn't. Reality is crystal clear to such a person.

- Comfortable acceptance of self, others, and nature: Self-actualizer don't keep organizing pity parties around their inadequacies or condemning those of others. They simply accept these shortcomings and focus on the important stuff.

- Reliant on own experiences and judgement: Self-actualizers don't give into 'thinking as a group'. They think for themselves, regardless of the culture and environment in which they find themselves.

- Task centering: Their lives are centered on the fulfillment of certain tasks or responsibilities that are beyond themselves.

- Autonomy: With these individuals, their lives and actions aren't dependent on other people. Independence is a key feature of self-actualizers.

- The continued freshness of appreciation: Unlike others, the self-actualizer is not blind to the beauty in his/her environment; little things such as the sunset and flowers are intensely appreciated over and over again.

- Profound interpersonal relationships: Self-actualizers seem to form better relationships than other people, and these relationships are usually very deep and meaningful.

- Comfort with solitude: For you to be a self-actualizer, you must be comfortable with being by yourself. Solitude is never a threat for a self-actualizer.

- The non-hostile sense of humor: Self-actualizers have the ability to laugh at themselves when they make mistakes.

- Peak experiences: Self-actualizers usually have feelings of being at one with the world around them, and these experiences are so deep that they are called peak experiences.

- Few friends: Self-actualizers tend to have a couple of intimate friends as opposed to a lot of superficial relationships.

**Cognitive Dissonance**

An interesting theory was proposed by renowned psychologist, Leon Fistenger who proposed a theory called cognitive dissonance. According to this theory, whenever we are in disharmony with ourselves it's actually because our behavior and beliefs are inconsistent. If you are unhappy with your life it is because your life is not the way you once saw it in your mind.

Even if others around you think that you are in a good place, you aren't quite satisfied because you haven't gotten to where you want to be. The truth, however, is that you are where you are right now because at some point you lost control of your thoughts. Your thoughts, much like children require constant supervision. Our thoughts are tremendously powerful. The Bible says in Proverbs 23:7, "As a man thinketh in his heart so is he.". In effect, you will go as far as your thoughts allow you to.

It's time to think in a new way, to have a paradigm shift in thinking; so that you can become crystal clear on what exactly you want. You have to envision your life as you would like it to be. So let's make this as practical as possible: Take a moment. Close your eyes; take in a deep breath and think about your life. Are you waking up with the sun at 9:00 am or are you getting up at 6:00 am and heading downstairs to your home gym for an early morning workout session. Are you heading over to work this morning or do you work from home? Did you wake up next to your husband/wife or did you wake up alone? What did you eat for breakfast? Did you prepare a huge meal for yourself;

complete with buttermilk pancakes topped with fresh berries drizzled in maple syrup with scrambled egg whites and 3 slices of turkey bacon? Or did you wake up this morning to the smell of freshly brewed coffee, slip on your favorite silk robe and head downstairs where you find your husband... He hands you a cup of coffee with a smile in your favorite "hello gorgeous" coffee mug no less and a freshly baked croissant from that bakery you love around the corner? That sure sounds great to me, but I did all of that for you to get the point, which is that in order for you to create the vision, you'll need the help of as many of your 5 senses as possible. It's not enough to want something, you have to become very specific and detail oriented. What did the pancakes taste like? Can you smell the coffee? How did the silk robe feel against your skin? These details matter because they help you to create a mental picture in your mind and if you don't get to the point where you see it with your mind; you'll never see it with your eyes. Visualizing the life you want is the key to getting the life you want. Merriam-Webster dictionary defines visualization as the act or process of interpreting in visual terms or of putting into visible form. Simply put, a good imagination can fool your brain.

Alexander Graham Bell once said, "What this power is I cannot say; all I know is that it exists and it becomes available only when a man is in that state of mind in which he knows exactly what he wants and is fully determined not to quit until he finds it."

The reason visualization is so important is because, without it, you will lack the needed motivation to do the work necessary to achieve your goal. For example, if you would love to lose 20-30 pounds but you are unable to mentally see yourself 20-30 pounds lighter, you won't be motivated to get up early and go to the gym. You won't have the discipline to skip dessert for a month. Visualization is not about you having that thing you've always wanted some time in the future, it is about feeling the feelings of having that thing now. It's not about imagining yourself a year from now having lost the 20-30 pounds but feeling as if you've already lost it RIGHT NOW. Visualization doesn't postpone stuff; it is about bringing your dreams into the present and taking them out of the future where they feel like they're too far off your reach. Practically, how do you get into this point of visualization? Through proper use of your thoughts. Your thoughts are the catalyst that activates the ideas and triggers the brain to creatively determine the best way of actualizing those thoughts and visions, thus making them tangible.

Our thoughts are so powerful! Everything starts with a thought. Seeing your life the way you would like it to be must become a daily ritual for you. For visualization to be most effective, becoming totally obsessed with your vision must become a necessity. Sports reporter Ahmad Rashad interviewed iconic basketball legend Michael Jordan several years after his retirement. Ahmad asked Jordan to speak about the infamous "game six". Michael says, "I practice as if I'm playing the game. So when the moment comes in the game, it's not new to me." In the now world-famous game, while being heavily guarded, Jordan shakes his defender and sinks the shot. This further drives home the point that visualization is mental practice. It makes you prepared such that you instinctively know how to handle the enormity of that moment when it does arrive, without you having to make such an effort.

Make a conscious choice to carve out a few minutes every day to focus your energy on the vision you've created. Creating the vision is only the beginning. You must also have the feeling. How would it feel to be in your dream relationship? How would it feel to get the job you've always wanted? How would it feel to buy your dream home? Visualization, if done properly, should be a 3 part exercise. First, you believe. Then you imagine. And finally, you feel. Each part is equally as important as the other. Your dream is almost like a dormant volcano. It's always been within you but it will only erupt under optimal conditions. Dr. Norman Vincent Peale is quoted as saying, "Formulate and stamp indelibly on your mind a mental picture of yourself as succeeding. Hold this picture tenaciously and never permit it to fade. Your mind will seek to develop this picture!" Need Examples? There are countless stories of successful people utilizing the power of visualization to turn their dreams into reality. Take UFC Champion fighter Conor McGregor for example. In 2013, he had absolutely nothing but by 2015, he had everything. In those two years, Conor trained religiously. He also believed and visualized himself as the UFC champion and that's exactly what he became. In the post-Championship press conference following McGregor's victory in 2015, a reporter stands up and asks, "I was asking you on Thursday about his right hand. Can I tell you what you told me?" Conor replies, "I said his right hand would get him into trouble. It's the shot I predicted...". Utterly astonished by the accuracy of McGregor's prediction the reporter asks in disbelief, "How do you do that?" Conor replies, "If you can see it here, and have the courage enough to speak it, it will happen." Billionaire media mogul Oprah Winfrey says, "Create the highest, grandest vision possible for your life because you become what you believe." Will Smith is also a firm believer in the power of visualization. He once said, "In my mind, I've always been an A-list Hollywood superstar. Y'all just didn't know yet."

This boils down to one point, if you want to be successful: You have to change the way you see yourself. Speaking positively about one's self comes easier to some than to others. If it almost feels unnatural for you to say out loud what you want, you have to work on your negative self-talk.

If you are attempting to elevate your thoughts and create a vision for your life and you're met with internal resistance, you have to resolve those issues before you can advance to the next step. It may be necessary for you to reprogram your way of thinking. You'll be forced to make a choice. You can keep doing what you've always done and continue getting what you've always gotten. Or you can begin to think differently and open your mind to a whole new realm of possibilities. Old thinking has never, and will never open new doors. You must make a concerted effort to silence your inner critic… that little voice in your head that is always telling you why you cannot do something because it's too late, you're too old, you're not pretty enough, smart enough, skinny enough, you don't have the education to do that, no one with your past could do this, you don't have the money for this or that.

The truth is that you deserve every good thing this life has to offer you. However, you have to be completely convinced of this or either consciously or subconsciously you will sabotage your own best efforts. For example, if you don't honestly believe you deserve that amazing guy you've been dreaming of, you'll find a way to push him away just so that you can confirm to yourself, "See, I knew no one would love me." You've got your work cut out for you, and it is to silence any voice that would attempt to limit you or your beliefs. Sometimes the critic is in your mind and sometimes it's other people attempting to project their doubts, fears, and insecurities onto you.

In 1990, a relatively unknown black girl from Compton, California is being interviewed. She says in a very matter of fact way, "I know I can beat her." Somewhat taken aback by this newcomers self-assuredness the reporter says, "Day One. Very confident." The girl replies with a smile, "I am very confident." Clearly doubting her, the reporter says, "You say it so easily. Why?" Before the girl could answer the girl's father emerges from the background and interrupts. He walks from the shadows and says, "alright cut right there. And let me tell you why. What she just said. She said it with so much confidence the first time. But you keep going on and on." The reporter unsuccessfully tries to interject, "but we can't keep interrupting. I mean -if you want" Abruptly cut off again by the young girl's father the man says, "you've got to understand that you're dealing with the image of a 14-year-old child...When she say something, we done told you what's happening. You're dealing with a little black kid, let her be a kid. She done answer it with a lot of confidence. Leave that alone!" The young girl went on to win 49 singles titles and

22 doubles titles. You may have heard of her, Venus Williams. Venus's younger sister Serena Williams is on the verge of breaking women's tennis history. Serena has won 22 majors, just two major championship wins away from tying all-time record holder Margaret Court. Although Richard William's methods may not have been popular or even conventional, you cannot help but respect how vigorously he protected the fragile psyche of this teenage girl from a long forgotten part of the country who dared to dream and believe in herself against all odds.

We all have a lesson to learn from him. To protect the vision you have created for your life, it may be necessary for you to be equally as brazen and unapologetic in defense of your dreams. You may have to interrupt someone mid-sentence if they attempt to speak against the vision you've worked so hard to create. It may also be necessary for you to end or suspend certain relationships in your life. Whatever it takes for you to divorce your old way of thinking and adopt a new one, you've got to get it done. Become radical about what you believe in, and be prepared to defend and protect that belief with every fiber of your being.

"Small minds cannot comprehend big spirits. To be great you have to be willing to be mocked, hated and misunderstood. Stay strong" -Robert Tew.

It's important to note that even while in the process of believing, imaging and having the feeling of the life you have envisioned, you must still be grounded enough and present enough to be grateful for where you are. If you constantly delay happiness until you're married, living in your dream home, finished writing your next book, starting your own business etc. you'll be surprised to discover that when you get there, you feel nothing. You will feel nothing because the moment may never be as grand as you have made it out to be in your mind. So you must enjoy this journey which is called life, every single moment of it. A few months ago I read the book, "The Alchemist" by Paulo Coelho. In the book, there is a story within a story. A shopkeeper sends his son to learn the secret of happiness from the wisest man in the world. The boy traveled 40 days before arriving at the beautiful castle where the wise man lived. He waited two hours to finally get an opportunity to speak with the wise man. Although the wise man listened attentively to the boy's request, he was unable to explain the secret to happiness to the boy at that time and so in the meantime, he requested that the boy take a look around his beautiful castle. He gave him a teaspoon with two drops of oil and instructed him not to spill it. Sometime later the boy returns to the wise man with the spoonful of oil intact. The man asked him what he thought of his beautiful castle. The boy confesses that he had been so consumed with not spilling the oil that he didn't take time to notice. So the man asked the boy to tour the castle again. This time the boy was attentive and noticed every detail. The beautiful tapestries, the pristine garden, the library etc. Everything was magnificent! When the boy returned to the wise man this time he was excited and recalled all of the beautiful things he had seen. The wise man was pleased but asked, "what about the oil?" In the boy's enthusiasm, he had spilled the oil. The wise man used this to illustrate to the boy that there is nothing wrong with being laser focused on something but to also take the time to appreciate the beauty of everything that surrounds you. We miss out on so many beautiful moments in pursuit of better ones. It has been said that tomorrow is the most dangerous word there is. It lulls us into a false sense of security, encourages us to settle and makes us embrace the mediocrity of our current life. Tomorrow is a thief because it robs you of the opportunity to share your gifts and become the best version of yourself now. Spiritual teacher Eckhart Tolle says this, "Most humans are never fully present in the now because unconsciously they believe that the next moment must be more important than this one. But then you miss your whole life, which is never not now." Enjoy every day because whether you do or you don't, it'll fade quickly and tomorrow will be right in your face.

# CHAPTER 2
## *Finding Your Purpose*

Motivational speaker, best-selling author, and preacher, the late Dr. Myles Munroe, once said, "The wealthiest place in the world is not the gold mines of South America or the oilfields of Iraq or Iran. They are not the diamond mines of South Africa or the banks of the world. The wealthiest place on the planet is just down the road. It is the cemetery. There lie buried companies that were never started, inventions that were never made, bestselling books that were never written, and masterpieces that were never painted. In the cemetery is buried the greatest treasure of untapped potential." He went on to say, "The greatest tragedy in life is not death, but a life without a purpose." We all possess what multimillionaire, businessman and rapper JayZ calls "genius level talent."

Sadly, we often discount and dismiss our purpose because we don't feel there's something about us that's special enough to be shared with the world. You look at some of the world's most powerful and influential people in history (past and present) and see that their purpose or calling touched the hearts and lives of millions. The Kings', The Gandhi's', The Nelson Mandelas' of this world. You may doubt that you possess that certain "it" factor that makes you unique.

Well, if the world didn't need you, you wouldn't be here. You were created because there was a void in the Earth that only you could fill, whether you believe it or not. We all didn't need to make it our life's mission to fight against inequality and end segregation. We all didn't need to be imprisoned for 27 years to stand against apartheid in South Africa. And we all didn't need to help India gain its independence from Great Britain and improve relations between Hindus and Muslims. But maybe you're a great listener, writer, singer or poet. Your purpose may not sound important enough or life-changing to you, but only if you compare it to someone else's. Theodore Roosevelt once said, "Comparison is the thief of joy". No, you may not discover the cure for cancer or end world hunger but that doesn't mean your gift is not important and the world is not eagerly waiting for you to share that special gift which is wrapped within you, and which only you can give. We were all created for a reason. There are two most important days of one's life; the day we were born and the day we realize why we were born. Purpose is the key that unlocks every door. My belief is that you will never experience true happiness until you discover that reason and walk in your divine purpose. I think people often overlook their purpose because they don't think their purpose is special enough.

According to Forbes, at least 70% of people hate their jobs, yet they appear each morning and probably work from 9-5. This goes a long way to show that many people need to step up on doing what they really love, instead of just appearing at jobs which they obviously hate.

No matter what you do and which path you choose to follow in life, if you don't find your purpose you might as well have wasted your existence. Finding your purpose is what gives your life meaning and makes it worth living. The journey to discovering that purpose could take years or it could be something you've known all your life, it varies for each individual. Discovering your purpose is really about finding your who, what, when, where and how. Whether you've noticed it or not, your purpose has been leaving you subtle clues all of your life. You know instinctively that you were destined to do more and to be more than you are right now. If you've ever asked yourself questions like, "what am I destined to do" "what makes me unique" "why am I even here" or "what is my purpose" this chapter was written to assist you in answering those questions and to help you gain a better perspective. But first, get yourself a piece of paper, a pen and search for the quietest corner you can find and write down your answers to the following questions:

⇒ What am I naturally good at?
⇒ What is that one thing that I do that I lose track of time when I'm doing?
⇒ What is it that I do best with the least amount of effort?
⇒ How do I spend my weekends?
⇒ If I won the lottery what would I still be doing?
⇒ What have I been doing since I was a child?
⇒ What am I doing when I'm at my happiest?

Based on your answers to the previous questions, write your own personal mission statement. Writing a personal mission statement is putting your vision or goal for your life into writing. Don't worry about whether or not that 'something' seems like a realistic career or not. Just answer honestly. Here are a few examples;

"To inspire women to know their worth and reach their highest level of greatness through my books and coaching."

"To travel the world, experience different cultures and document my experiences for all the world to see."

"To share healthy, hearty and tasty vegan recipes and showcase the amazingness of plant-based foods."

"To motivate young and disadvantaged children to finish high school and attend college."

"To heal the hearts and minds of battered women and to help them regain their sense of self-worth and restore their dignity."

"To create an app that gives undiscovered artists a platform to share their work with the world."

"To brighten the day of children suffering from terminal illnesses such as cancer with comedy and music."

"To write books for little black girls on embracing their natural hair and physical features and help them to see the beauty in the way they were created."

Maybe your mission statement is to be independently wealthy, live in a beautiful estate in Vermont and make jam like Olivia Pope. Whether you're doing what you love in the evenings after work, on the weekends or every day for a living, you will be happier when you are doing more of what you love. Once you have discovered your purpose, your next logical step is to determine if you can do it for a living. Now let's address the elephant in the room, money! Not everyone living their purpose will be rich but it's not outside of the realm of possibility to expect your gift, talent or purpose to support you.

Some people feel uncomfortable charging a fee for their natural God-given ability. But it is necessary if you ever want to live in your purpose exclusively and not have a 9 to 5 job, that leaves you feeling empty and drained. The word talent is derived from the Latin word talentum which means the sum of money. In other words, you should expect to be compensated for sharing your gift and shouldn't feel guilty about providing a service that you genuinely love and which enriches the lives of those with whom you share that gift.

Successful people always leave clues, so see if there's someone with a similar purpose and study what they've done. This is not so that you can replicate what they've done and dilute your own uniqueness but to see if there's already a market for what you have to offer. Consider getting a mentor to help you get better established. This is not the time to be general but to be specific. If you want to make couture clothing for your poodles to be sold in high-end dog boutiques, studying the career of a highly successful pastry chef won't do you much good. However, if you are unable to be mentored by someone, invest in yourself and your future. Watch their interviews, read their books, attend their seminars. Become a student. As the saying goes, "when the student is ready the master appears."

When you have found your purpose, you no longer feel like you are losing or betraying yourself. You know when you're on a job that you hate and you know that you are destined for something greater, it doesn't feel right. For the life of you, you can't shake this nagging feeling that this is wrong and not where you're supposed to be. On the outside, when you take a sneak peek at your feelings, they don't quite make sense. You may be making a decent living, with a very respectable title and in the beautiful corner office you've always dreamed of but it feels like a hollow victory. You're supposed to be happy and fulfilled but you've never felt emptier!

The truth is, when you are walking in your purpose you won't feel like the cost is greater than the reward. When you are doing something that is not in line with your purpose; it doesn't matter how much they're paying you, it will never be enough because purpose isn't about money- it is about a feeling. There is no greater feeling than knowing you are exactly where you need to be and doing exactly what you were created to do. That's a tremendous sense of completeness and wholeness that nothing else can duplicate. Purpose is magnetic; it draws you like a moth to a flame. It's what ignites the fire within you. Purpose goes hand in hand with passion. When you are truly passionate about something you can lose all track of time. When you are doing what you love and were created to do, it is the first thing you think about when you wake up in the morning and the last thing you think about when you go to bed at night. It is that fire in your belly which cannot be extinguished.

Once you've discovered your purpose then it's time to explore your creativity. It's a very interesting dichotomy. You'll need to be general yet specific at the same time. Sometimes it is necessary for you to expand the vision but the key is to do so while remaining true to the original purpose. Take Steve Jobs for example, his purpose was innovation and technology. He didn't just limit himself to one specific medium for that gift. He created the iPhone, the iPad, Apple Tv, Macbook etc. He gave himself the freedom to explore while remaining true to his original gift. You will have to possess a willingness to go wherever purpose takes you. One of the most common misconceptions when it comes to purpose it that it will make you rich. That's not an untrue statement; however, the belief that becoming rich as a result of your purpose is what makes you happy is not true. You will soon discover that there are things far more important than money. Make no mistake; money is not a bad thing. So many people misquote the scripture 1 Timothy 6:10. It is not money is the root of all evil but, "for the love of money is the root of all evil". Money buys medicine, clean water, feeds the hungry etc. but it is only evil when someone would do anything to get it. You don't actually need the big house, the fancy car or the huge bank account, what you really want is the feeling you would get from those things. None of those things can guarantee you happiness, as a matter of fact, it's only your purpose that can do that. Don't pursue money, instead pursue purpose. Regardless of what you've been made to believe, money doesn't equate happiness. Rather, the more you do what you love the happier you will be.

What no one ever tells you about purpose and following your dreams:
- ⇒ Purpose is hard work.
- ⇒ Purpose will cost you something. (invest time, money and energy)
- ⇒ Purpose may cost you the love and support of family and friends.
- ⇒ Purpose pushes you past your comfort zone.

True purpose is about service to others. It is not self-serving. This isn't about you becoming rich and famous although that does happen in some instances. In those cases, the money and fame help to serve even more people and the philanthropic efforts become greater and on an even broader scale.

Twain said, "The harder I worked the luckier I became." You may have already discovered your gift but now you're wondering how exactly you can afford to live your dream. How can you afford not do? Can you be paid to do whatever it is that you truly love? How does it serve you to live a life void of passion? Living a purpose driven life is not just a career change it's a lifestyle. Who says you can't profit from your purpose or talent? One of the common mistakes people make is assuming that because that thing they're truly passionate about isn't as common as say, singing, dancing, writing etc. that they can't do it for a living. Snap out of it, and think out of the box! If your talent isn't a typical job that doesn't mean it can't be.

You could inspire others around you to walk in your footsteps by pioneering a new movement, who knows? So get up, and follow your passion.

Let me be clear. Following your passion doesn't necessarily mean you should quit your day job. If you're in a position where you can afford to, by all means go for it! However, if you must remain gainfully employed, at least for the moment, use some of the money to invest in your vision, learn what you can from your job, and to trust the process. Everything you've ever done and experienced is preparing for the next stage in your life.

Take my story for example. For two years, I worked as a Quality Management Coordinator handling customer complaints and writing letters on behalf of a multimillion-dollar company. I hated it! At the time, I couldn't see what writing letters had to do with my gift or calling. My passion has always been inspiring, uplifting and encouraging women to know their worth and live their best lives. Listening to people complain all day seemed like a tremendous waste of time. Now I realize in those two years I was honing my writing skills and being prepared to become an author. I also spent two years working as an instructor at a local community college. Before accepting the position I struggled with public speaking. But, after spending two years teaching adults not only was I comfortable with public speaking, I grew to love it. At the time, I didn't see what teaching aspiring dental assistants had to do with my gift. I realize now that job prepared me to be a motivational speaker by giving me the skills and confidence to speak in front of hundreds of people.

Let's take Oprah Winfrey for example. Being a talk show host wasn't common back in her day. As a matter of fact, when she first started out, she was fired from her job because she was said to be too "emotionally involved" with the stories she reported. But Oprah is an intrinsically emotional woman; as she went on to show the world by creating her own TV show and being herself on the Oprah Winfrey Show. With this unique thing about her, coupled with a lot of hard work, Oprah has become a household name today, with her net worth being over $2.9 billion dollars. Being a news reporter may not have felt like it was a part of Oprah's calling or purpose at the time, but she was being prepared.

# CHAPTER 3
## Watch Your Mouth

Negative words become self-fulfilling prophecies. You are the result of what you've believed, the choices you've made and what you have said about yourself. It's easy to look around and assign blame elsewhere. Too many of us try to blame our parents. Maybe your parents insisted you go to law school or become a doctor instead of fulfilling your dream of becoming an artist. They told you, "Make us proud" and up till now, you have dedicated your entire life to doing just that. Sometimes it's our family and friends that are the first ones to talk us out of doing what we are most passionate about. " We know they love us, want the best for us and their opinions are coming from a good place. But no one ever bothered to ask you what you want to do with your own life.

Steve Jobs said, "Don't waste your life living someone else's life." You shouldn't expect those who have never pursued their own dreams to be in support of your decision to pursue yours! So, you decide to do what everyone wants you to, while being secretly jealous of all those who dared to follow their own inner compass and live their best lives on their own terms.

Hey, you don't have to keep on living like that! You can live your dream too, if you stop making excuses! You have to develop a "no matter what" mentality. Successful people already have this mentality and that is what fuels their success. They weren't necessarily more intelligent or even more talented than you or anyone else, but they were more determined and more dedicated. They probably had the same excuses as you did but they blatantly refused to let those excuses keep them from walking in their destinies or to prevent them from realizing their full potential.

In order for you to go from where you are now to where you want to be, you will have to face some hard truths. The first truth is that it's really no one's fault that you are where you are but your own. Every choice you've made has contributed to where you find yourself now. Rather than dispute this indisputable fact, be honest with yourself and begin to revamp your choices. What do you say about yourself? Did you ever think, "I can never do that" "that kind of thing happens to other people but never to someone like me" "I'm a failure" or "I wish I were her"? Those are not questions that should ever be on your lips. Just because you failed once doesn't make you a failure. Realize that your life is bigger than this one moment. In life, you are always being prepared for the next journey. So instead of asking yourself "why me" consider asking yourself "what was this here to teach me?". There is always a lesson to be learned from every painful situation, so learn the lesson and get ready for life's next test. These are not obstacles but opportunities. If you've been down on yourself for so long that it has become uncomfortable for you to start speaking positively about yourself -tell yourself a lie until you begin to believe it. Remember when you were a child and you used to use your imagination? You could become whatever you thought you were. You would play with your doll and pretend you were a mom. You would put on a plastic stethoscope and just like that, you had become a doctor. You would place a crown on the top of your head and now suddenly you were a princess. The point I'm making here is that the child version of yourself was trying to teach you something – that your dreams can be bigger than your present reality. You could become whatever you believed yourself to be. However, somewhere along the way you became afraid and got overtaken by feelings of inadequacy and self-doubt. You became used to the darkness. One of my favorite movies of all time is "Dark Knight Rises" with Christian Bale. There is a scene where Batman is being broken by the antagonist in the story, Bane.

While beating him down physically, Bane also attempts to break him emotionally by saying this, "You think darkness is your ally. But you've merely adopted the dark. I was born in it. Molded by it. I didn't see the light until I was already a man and by then it did nothing to me but blind me." Never get so used to the darkness that it becomes as familiar as an old friend. That would mean that you were beginning to welcome it secretly, and possibly, you are even slightly comforted by it. You were never meant to live your life in the darkness but to be surrounded by the light.

While reading this book you may feel as if you've hit rock bottom and that's ok because rock bottom is a great place to rebuild your foundation and start again. What you are experiencing is resistance. To overcome resistance you have to do 3 things:

First, you must acknowledge and eliminate your excuses. To do this, you must be truly honest with yourself. For example, you can't say you don't have time to work on your dreams when you've binge-watched season after season of "The Big Bang Theory" on Netflix. Can you be found every Thursday night watching "Grey's Anatomy", "Scandal" and "How To Get Away With Murder"? Shonda Rimes Thursday night lineup of shows is the stuff that dreams are made of. But, couldn't those three hours be better spent working on your business plan, writing a chapter in the book you've always wanted to write or a taking an online course that can earn you the promotion at work. Your favorite actors on your favorite television shows are already living their dreams. Don't let television distract you from living yours. If television is taking up too much of your time turn it off. The life you want to live will require some sacrifice. We make time for the things we deem important. Isn't living a life doing what you really love to do worth some of your free time? If you didn't think so, you would not be reading this book.

Next, stop procrastinating and start taking action. Are you one of those people that thinks New Year's resolutions don't work? Perhaps it's because the goal is clear but your timetable is not. Break your ultimate goal into bite-sized pieces. What can you do today or this week that will get you closer to where you want to be? For example, if you love to travel but you've never left the United States. Maybe your first step is to go online and research the documents that you'll need to secure your passport tonight after work. Next week you can stop by the Post Office to get a passport application. By the end of the month, you should have you scheduled an appointment to get your passport photo taken and submitted your application. Once you receive your passport, you can begin looking into possible destinations and airline fares. When there is no timetable for completing your goals they rarely get done. Deadlines create a sense of urgency that eliminates procrastination. If you need a little help staying motivated, get an accountability partner that you can trust. If you don't have someone to help you be accountable, make a "to do" list and start with the smallest item on the list, working your way up to the largest task. Any progress is better than no progress at all.

Lastly, you must acknowledge that everything you need to be successful is already within you. You just have to tap into your potential. Marianne Williamson once said, "Our deepest fear is not that we are inadequate. Our deepest fear is that we are powerful beyond measure. It is our light, not our darkness that most frightens us. We ask ourselves, who am I to be brilliant, gorgeous, talented, fabulous? Actually, who are you not to be? You are a child of God. Your playing small does not serve the world. There is nothing enlightened about shrinking so that other people won't feel insecure around you. We are all meant to shine, as children do."

Get on your path to being whom you were made to be!

# CHAPTER 4
## *The Beauty Of Failures*

"Failure should be our teacher, not our undertaker. Failure is delay, not defeat. It is a temporary detour, not a dead end. Failure is something we can avoid only by saying nothing, doing nothing, and being nothing." - Denis Waitley

The above words spoken by Denis Waitley are wise words indeed, but it hasn't succeeded in eradicating the fear of failure in the hearts of many individuals. To date, many of us are content with allowing ourselves to be robbed of our chances of success for as long as possible. It is all too easy to forget that failure ought to be just a teacher in the heat of the moment, when battling with failure!

Sara Blakely, CEO of Spanx often shares the story of how her father would ask her and her brother every evening at the dinner table what they had failed at during the day. She went so far as to say that her father was visibly disappointed if she didn't have something to say she'd failed at that week. When she would mention to her father the things she failed at, he would celebrate the failure with a high-five. Of course, that rewired her mentally and Sara often says that it reframed her thinking about failure. Failure, for her, became more about not trying than about what the outcome would be.

"Fear kills more dreams than failure ever will."
- Suzy Chasm

The fear of failure can lead to self-sabotaging behavior. We sabotage our own successes when we procrastinate, cook up excuses, and inadvertently, when we are inactive. If these self-sabotaging attitudes are left unaddressed, they can keep one stuck in one place emotionally, physically, personally and professionally for a really long time. For example, if you wanted to lose twenty pounds but you've tried several weight loss plans over the years yet none of them have worked; you might be scared that no matter how hard you try, you still won't lose the weight. It wouldn't mean a thing that you'd joined a gym program a month earlier because you don't have a mindset that's already set in favor of weight loss. Without a willing mindset, you'll discover that you lack the will power to say no to your favorite high carb, high-fat comfort foods and just as you feared, you don't lose the weight. Mostly because you self-sabotaged by indulging in those foods.

Perhaps, you are the only one in your family to have gone to college and gotten your degree. You really want to get your master's degree but you're afraid that if you start making even more money, your family and friends will treat you differently and so, you don't apply for school in the fall. This is another really good example of self-sabotaging behavior.

Sometimes we sabotage ourselves because we are afraid of what our success would imply to other people and to the relationships in our lives. How would our friends react to our climb up the ladder of success? Would our relationships nose-dive if we were more successful? In our minds, we've created a certain narrative and we tell ourselves these stories that we do not know for sure are even true. Have you ever told yourself any one of these lies?

- I'm not smart enough to finish school
- I'll never get married
- No one will marry a woman who already has children
- I'll never own my own home
- I'm too awkward and weird for anyone to want to get to know me
- I'm not worthy of love
- I'm not going to be a good wife or mother
- My past will ruin my future

- I'm not good enough
- There's nothing special about me
- I only attract bad boys
- My parents will never be proud of me
- I'm too hard to love
- My dreams will never come true
- I'll always be in debt
- I'll never lose the weight
- I'm a failure

Take a moment to write down the specific lies that you've been telling yourself. Silencing your inner critic is not something you should do but something you must learn to do often. However, before you silence it, take a moment to listen to it and learn from it. If you fear success because you think you won't have time for your love life, you'll never have children, you'll become a workaholic, you'll lose all your friends, people will think you're crazy, you'll disappoint your parents etc. you have to acknowledge those fears before you can eliminate them. Accept that even if there's a possibility of any one of those things happening, you can eliminate the chances by working hard at it.

Next, you need to create a contradicting mantra. For example, if you have the negative thought that you only attract bad boys; your new mantra could be, "I am a magnet for healthy relationships". Do you have negative thoughts about your weight? Consider adopting the mantra, "I am becoming healthier and stronger every day". Overwhelmed by feelings of inadequacy? Try "I am enough". They aren't just words, but statements that would help change your reality, reframe your thoughts and bring you into a much better place.

Make a commitment to yourself. You can say: insert your name here, "I promise to always make time for the people and moments that matter most." Or whatever it is that was the fear that kept you from moving forward. The acronym for fear is false evidence appearing real. You may have conditioned yourself to feel like you don't deserve what you truly want and that's why you'll never have it. Therefore, the first step to turning your life around and creating positive change is to create that reality in your mind first. Whenever you feel afraid, that's an indication that you're on the way out of your comfort zone. The alarm bells go off and red lights start flashing and for a moment you freeze. You get a case of what Psychologist Barry Schwartz called: "analysis paralysis". We spend our time endlessly planning, troubleshooting and "preparing" while telling ourselves that we're just waiting for the perfect time and when that time comes, we'll have the right response straightaway. However, if you want to be like the great, you have to incorporate one of their traits, which is the ability to launch into things before you're ready. Perfectionism is often fear in disguise.

Failure isn't the end of the world. It is in fact, the best invitation to try again, because you might have to start all over, from scratch. It also affords you a great opportunity for learning. If you think about it in an unbiased manner, you might discover that you have learned more from your failures than you ever have from your successes. What failure does is to force you to stop being laid back or being lazy. Instead, it taps you, waking you up from your deep slumber and while you might not like that anymore than you like it when your alarm goes off every morning and you have to get up; it sets you on a journey towards the achievement of your dreams- but that's if you want it to go that way. This is the story of almost every successful person you have ever heard about, or read about.

Take for example, Henry Ford, who came from nothing and later revolutionized the entire car-making industry. At the age of 16, Ford left his father's farm to become a machinist apprentice in Detroit, working for the next couple of years in the car manufacturing industry. However, his first two companies collapsed and it was only on his third attempt that the Ford Motor Company was created, in 1903. This only became a reality possible because Ford didn't give up during any of those attempts and he later went on to manufacture nine successful car models. His cars were practical, affordable and innovative. Ford showed to the entire world that there was power in perseverance and that if you took a step at a time, you would get to where you have always wanted to.

How about Walt Disney? Walt Disney was fired by a newspaper editor because he was told that "he lacked imagination and had no good ideas." When he founded his first animation company in Kansas City, Walt didn't make a headway soon enough, from shipping cartoons to a company in New York and getting paid 6 months later, to all sorts of saddening jobs that he never expected he'd find himself doing. Tired and discouraged, Walt had to dissolve the company, reportedly having to survive on dog food because he couldn't afford his rent. When he got the idea of Mickey Mouse, he was told that it wouldn't do him any good, because "a giant mouse on the screen would terrify women". Look where the Walt Disney enterprise is today, and how far his imagination and belief in himself took him!

We are all familiar with Kentucky Fried Chicken, but no one believed in Colonel Sanders at first, as his chicken recipe was rejected over 1,000 times before it finally began to make him any profit. His was a classic case of complete rejection before being re-accepted.

Walt Disney and Colonel Sanders are no different from you. You just probably haven't tried as hard as they have or for as long as they have, and so if they could beat the odds and get to the top, no one should be able to stop you! In fact, when opportunities aren't being presented to you, you have to create them for yourself.

Every day, we have opportunities presented to us in the form of obstacles, and the key to winning in life is to choose to transform those obstacles into opportunities. As the saying goes, "when you change the way you look at things, the things you look at change."

I have found that to be true in my life, and so have the people who have gotten to great heights…you'll likely discover the same if you choose to change your perspective on those obstacles in your path…who knows, you might be on your way to materializing some genius idea that would totally shake the world!

Let me take a moment here to share a bit about my story. In a perfect world, I would have been approached by some huge publishing house like Simon & Schuster. They would have written me a six-figure advance check for my first book, "The Dating Game: How To Find Yourself While Looking For Mr. Right". Unfortunately or fortunately, that didn't happen. So, I started writing my book anyway. I knew what I wanted and I knew the "how" would emerge. Long story short, this book will be my third self-published book. My first book and my second, "Breaking the Man Code: The Key To Unlocking His Heart" are both Amazon.com best sellers. Much like the stories I mentioned before, when the opportunity didn't present itself to me, I created it for myself. A few years ago, I held a book launch party to celebrate the release of my first book. While at this event, I was having a conversation with one of the attendees. She said, "You should host a women's retreat". The idea of such a thing had never once crossed my mind but my curiosity was piqued. Based on that, I held a very impromptu and informal survey. I asked a crowd consisting of about seventy women, "Hey ladies, if I hosted a women's retreat, would any of you be interested?" The crowd answered with a deafening and unanimous, "yes!" Wow...for me that was completely revolutionary!

I knew nothing about hosting a retreat at the time but again I knew what I wanted and I was confident that the 'how' would emerge. I called the retreat, "High Heels High Standards" and it was a huge success. To date, there have been three retreats. The fourth High Heels High Standards event is scheduled for November 2017. We will be heading to Turks and Caicos and the Dominican Republic on a five day four night luxury cruise. Now, imagine what would have happened if I'd chosen to ignore what the lady said to me, and decided not to follow through on the idea of a women's retreat. I would either still be wondering if the thought could transform into something great, or I might even have forgotten about it completely.

I have a confession to make. The last thing I want to do is to lead you into thinking that I have always been confident and self-assured. In fact, nothing could be further from the truth. There have been many times throughout my career that I have felt like a complete fraud. Occasionally we all suffer from something called "imposter syndrome" and I am no exception. The phrase imposter syndrome was coined back in 1978 by clinical psychologists Dr. Pauline R. Clance and Suzanne A. Imes. Imposter syndrome is a nagging fear of being found out as a fake and a phony, and feeling as if you have fooled everyone into believing one is competent.

Last year I was asked to speak at a women's empowerment event. At the time, the complete list of women who would also be speaking at this event had not been fully determined. One morning I received an email from the event planner with a list of names and biographies of the other women who would be speaking. I had a mini meltdown! Joining me on this event would be a doctor, a self-made millionaire, best-selling authors and women who had previously graced the stage with some of my heroes. And then there was little old me. As far as I had gotten to in my career, in that moment, I felt like a fraud. How was I supposed to get up and give a speech after these incredibly confident and accomplished women had just done the same? What made me qualified to even be here? I'm not the only one who has felt this way. The late great Nobel Laureate Maya Angelou once said, "I have written 11 books, but each time I think, 'Uh oh, they're going to find out now. I've run a game on everybody, and they're going to find me out.'" During a 2016 interview with Time Out magazine, acclaimed actress Lupita Nyong'o said this, "What's it called when you have a disease and it keeps recurring? I go through [acute impostor syndrome] with every role. I think winning an Oscar may, in fact, have made it worse. Now I've achieved this, what am I going to do next? What do I strive for? Then I remember that I didn't get into acting for the accolades, I got into it for the joy of telling stories." The incomparable Meryl Streep is quoted as saying, "You think, "Why would anyone want to see me again in a movie? And I don't know how to act anyway, so why am I doing this?"' THE Meryl Streep! The imposter syndrome shows up when we are experiencing a moment of vulnerability and it plagues us with feelings of doubt and insecurity. Do you secretly think to yourself, 'I don't deserve success'? When your friends, family or peers compliment you, do you secretly think they're lying to you? Anyone who tells you they've never been afraid and they've never once doubted themselves is lying to both you and themselves. As you can see by the examples of successful people I've just mentioned, it happens to the best of us but that doesn't mean we should sit back and accept it. Make no mistake; the negative thoughts inspired by the imposter syndrome are not harmless. If you are not careful, they will rob you of your dreams and keep you playing small in life forever. If I had allowed those negative thoughts to take root in my mind, I would have found an excuse to cancel my speaking engagement. If I had done that, I would never have been able to see that even on a panel with such accomplished women I was still able to hold my own. Ok, now I'm being a bit too modest, I did better than just hold my own, I did great! There were so many women waiting to speak to me, buy my books and enthusiastically request that I ask sign their copies afterward. It was one of the most empowering experiences of my career! It is important for you to understand that imposter syndrome is a form of self-sabotage. To overcome it, you're going to have to reprogram those negative thoughts of inadequacy and replace them with more self-empowering thoughts of confidence and strength. Don't be afraid to call it out by its name. "I know that's you imposter syndrome!" The simple act of identifying and then immediately denouncing that negative thought diminishes its power. As we discussed earlier in this chapter, you must remain conscious of your internal narrative and be diligent about exposing the lies you've been telling yourself. And don't be afraid to toot your own horn. Not in a braggadocious way, and certainly not to others, but to remind yourself of who you truly are on a daily basis. Sometimes we forget who we are and what we've accomplished when we compare ourselves to what others have done. In the words of Theodore Roosevelt, "comparison is the thief of joy". There's nothing wrong with acknowledging and appreciating the talents and gifts which others possess, but it should never cause you to diminish or question your own gifts and talents. Heroes and mentors should serve as inspirations only. Do not allow them to serve as the tools by which you measure your success.

# CHAPTER 5
## *Toxic Relationships*

They say we are the average of the five people we surround ourselves with the most. You would think that possessing this knowledge would encourage us to surround ourselves with people who genuinely see our potential, believe in our dreams and those who have a positive influence over our lives. Unfortunately, that is not always the case. Sadly, relationships are one of the biggest reasons why we feel stuck.

When relationships are discussed, we often think in terms of romantic relationships- but these aren't the only type of relationship we can have. Toxic relationships don't have to be limited to our romantic relationships, but can also include relationships involving family members, friends as well as business relationships. Eventually, these relationships lead to extreme stress, depression, anxiety and have a negative impact on one's self-esteem and self-confidence. Often, these relationships leave us emotionally, mentally and even physically drained.

In toxic relationships, efforts are never reciprocated- one person always ends up feeling used by the other. The danger with these types of relationships is that they can readily creep up on you. Often, people who are in toxic relationships have moments when they wonder how they got into them in the first place!

Because of the danger of them creeping up on you, one of the best ways to avoid being endangered by these kinds of relationships is to identify the signs as early as possible.
Here are some signs that you may be in a toxic relationship:

- ⇒ Constant Drama
- ⇒ Repeated Disrespect
- ⇒ Lack of trust
- ⇒ Never ending criticism
- ⇒ Never accepts "no" for answer
- ⇒ Always Controlling
- ⇒ Passive aggressive
- ⇒ You're always giving and they're always taking
- ⇒ You can't be yourself around them
- ⇒ They blame you for everything
- ⇒ They treat your feelings like they're invalid
- ⇒ They use your past against you
- ⇒ They hold your relationship hostage
- ⇒ They are inconsistent with their affection
- ⇒ They are jealous of your other relationships
- ⇒ They want to monopolize your time
- ⇒ They try to isolate you from friends and family
- ⇒ They constantly guilt trip you
- ⇒ They constantly compare you to someone else

⇒ They exploit your insecurities

⇒ They are jealous

Even if you have accepted any one of these actions as normal, I am obliged to let you know that it is not healthy for a relationship to leave you feeling this way. It is easy to fall into an attitude of denial while in a toxic relationship, but you must first of all, create a new mindset for yourself if you want to exit this cycle of toxicity in your relationships, as one toxic relationship often leads to another until it becomes a vicious cycle. The first step in getting unstuck from toxic relationships it to first admit that it is toxic. Think about the people who are closest to you, the people you spend the most time with. How do you feel when you are around them? Do any of the signs mentioned above apply to your relationship with them? If so, don't give them an excuse. It doesn't matter if the people these apply to be your parents, husband, boyfriend, fiancé, boss, best friend, sister etc. No one can make you feel like you are unworthy or unloved without your permission, and you should never permit anyone to make you feel this way about yourself. So, ask yourself, why are you granting someone permission to treat you in this way and feel like they have the right to do so? As a matter of fact, they should not remain in your life!

In this chapter, we will discuss two of the most common reasons we stay in toxic relationships and how we can get out of them.

**Reason #1: Familiarity & Nostalgia**

Those who are closest to you can sometimes be the most toxic. I acknowledge the fact that this is sad, but it's true. Those whom you trust the most and who ought to be there for you at all times might not be. Toxic relationships that are based on familiarity are ones where you feel that the other person has your best interests at heart, even when there is contradictory evidence such as; constant negativity, being controlling or dismissive. I need you to imagine if you can see yourself in any of the scenarios below:

Your mother was never married and based on her past experiences; she has a very poor opinion of men. You've been dating your boyfriend for almost a year now and things are starting to get serious. Your mother has never taken the time to get to know him (or any other boyfriend for that matter) but she doesn't like him. In fact, she's been very vocal about not liking any of your boyfriends. She's constantly telling you that he's gonna find someone else, cheat on you and then leave you. Deep down inside, you feel like your mother has intentionally sabotaged every relationship you've ever had. As a result of her years of negativity about men, she's made you question if any man would ever truly love you? How has that helped you? No, it hasn't! Instead, it has prevented you from climbing great heights because of a negative mentality that was passed on to you from a loved one who thinks your experiences would mirror hers.

Because the loved one is your mother, best friend, boyfriend etc.; you never considered this type of behavior as controlling or destructive, but it is. The loved one in question could have the best intentions in the world, but it's not about their intentions as much as it is about how their words and behavior make you feel. Those who are closest to you have the ability to easily disarm you and infiltrate your defenses. There's nothing you can do about that because that's the way it's designed to be. However, because their controlling ways are easily hidden by "I'm just looking out for you" "I just don't want you to make the same mistakes I did" or "I just want the best for you", it makes it harder to detect wrong attitudes and behaviors that might be having negative impact on you.

The best step to take would be to address any behavior which damages your self-confidence or makes you question your worth.

**Reason #2: Fear**

When toxic people identify what you fear, they exploit that fear in order to manipulate you. Often, we stay in toxic relationships out of the fear of loneliness, the fear of change, fear of losing loved ones, the fear of rejection and the fear of losing our security. We all have an intrinsic need or desire to feel secure in our homes, our jobs, and our relationships. When this sense of security is threatened, it becomes easier to accept unacceptable behavior in an attempt to hold on to what we feel we need or cannot live without. Take the scenarios below for example;

Your husband/partner is the primary breadwinner in your family. You have very little education, have only ever worked minimum wage jobs, and have small children at home. Whenever your boyfriend, fiancé or husband gets upset with you or wants you to do something, he reminds you that you could never make it on your own. And without him, you and your children would struggle financially. He has become controlling, jealous and disrespectful but you feel like you have no choice but to stay with him. Not because you are in love with him but because you're afraid of what life would be like without him. He has convinced you that you could never make it on your own. You start to believe that he is the best you can do. But really, is this the truth?

You have a co-worker or boss who is very disrespectful and tends to project blame on you for everything that goes wrong. You're not in a position where you can quit this job. So, you stay and take the verbal and emotional abuse because you are afraid of the unknown. Toxic people identify your fear of starting over or being on your own and turn it into a very harmful weapon.

Toxic relationships are like an addiction, and to break free of them will require a detox. It would also require genuine dedication and commitment to change. This can't be something which you think you should do but rather, something which you must do. I believe it was Buddha that said, "Anything that costs you your peace is too expensive."

The first step in detoxifying yourself from a toxic relationship is the creation of distance from that individual/ those individuals. This doesn't have to be a geographical distance; it could just be limiting or eliminating altogether your contact with the toxic individual. Making the decision to limit or eliminate contact is not about the other person as much as it is about self-preservation. You should never have to feel guilty for prioritizing self-care. Perhaps you're familiar with the oxygen mask analogy. If you've ever been on a flight, you've heard the flight attendant give their safety briefing. They always say something along the lines of, "In the unlikely event of a sudden loss of cabin pressure, oxygen masks will drop down from the panel above your head... Secure your own mask before helping others." Essentially, that's what you're doing by distancing yourself from a toxic individual; you are increasing your own odds of survival. Distancing yourself from a loved one or romantic partner can be difficult because you are still hopeful that they can and will change. It could also be that over the years, due to a myriad of circumstances, they have transformed from the loving individual that they once were and are now very toxic. Because of this, you might still be hopeful that they'd soon return back to the person they once were. You have to come to the realization that in spite of whom they once were, this is how the relationship is NOW. It does not serve you to live in the past, only the present. Distancing should also mean detaching. Remove them from your social media networks, decline their invitations to spend time together and don't answer their calls. This may seem harsh but if your sense of value and self-worth has been severely damaged by them, it's your responsibility to stop it, by any means necessary.

Moving on from a toxic relationship can be especially difficult if you are not aware of your triggers. For example, you tend to feel lonely around the holidays and that's when you are around your toxic family member; this could trigger a reuniting with someone who you had otherwise cut contact with. Perhaps you're used to cuddling with your significant other at night. During the day you are able to be strong and resist the urge to contact the toxic individual. However, during the night time, it is extremely difficult for you to remain vigilant.

This gives rise to step number two. Step number two in detoxifying yourself from a toxic relationship is to distract yourself especially when you're triggered. If you don't, you could easily fall back into old behaviors. Establish a new routine without them that makes you feel empowered. This is not an excuse for you to indulge in negative and destructive thoughts and behaviors such as overeating, assuming all the blame, giving up on love or isolating yourself from the people who love you. Take this time to do what makes you happy. If you love to paint, then start painting more. If you love to travel plan more weekend trips. Discover what makes you happy outside of that toxic person. When you attempt to leave a toxic relationship (and they know you're serious) this is often when they finally start saying what you've always wanted them to say or behaving in the way you've desired them to behave all along. This makes it even harder to walk away because there's a chance that the change they are demonstrating is real. Do not allow second thoughts, doubt or regret to creep into your mind. Although making the decision to move one may have been a difficult decision, it was a necessary one.

"Surround yourself with people who make you happy. People who make you laugh, who help you when you're in need. People who genuinely care. They are the ones worth keeping in your life. Everyone else is just passing through." - Karl Marx

Your relationships should nourish feelings of trust, respect, and love not anxiety, stress, and feelings of inadequacy. If you feel like you cannot break free of this toxic relationship on your own, don't be afraid or ashamed to get support from the people in your life that you trust. Consider getting an accountability partner. All too often we suffer in silence because we're scared that if we tell someone about the behavior we've been tolerating, they will judge us. Don't let fear be your excuse to stay where you are. Often, if the person you contact to help you is truthful enough, they might even let you in on some negative things that they also endured from other people in the past and then, you'd know that you aren't alone. You deserve to be genuinely happy and anyone in your life that does not contribute to that happiness should not be permitted to stay. It's that simple. Moving on will be hard but the pain won't last forever! The reward of getting your smile, your confidence and the boost to your self-esteem will be well worth it and when you look back, you would know that you made the right decision.

# CHAPTER 6

## *The Secret To Making Better Decisions*

I'm sure every person has asked themselves at least once in their lives, 'how did I get here?'. The answer is gradually. You probably woke up one day, took a good look at your life and were astonished at how far away you are from those great dreams you had and it feels like it all happened suddenly. No, nothing happens suddenly... you got here gradually, taking baby steps until you were on the curb! Where you are currently in your life is not the result of one big decision but rather the result of many small decisions taken over time. Therefore, changing your life will require you to make micro changes daily. We are the result of what we do every day.

This is why I would strongly encourage you to establish a morning ritual, and by that, I mean a series of actions performed repeatedly, every single day. John C. Maxwell says, "You will never change your life until you change something you do daily. The secret of your success is found in your daily routine."

How can you create a morning ritual? Well, I have some news for you and the news is that whether you are aware of it or not, you already have a morning ritual. The question is; does your morning ritual promote chaos or productivity? Does your current ritual leave you feeling stressed and mentally exhausted or refreshed and calm? When your alarm goes off in the morning do you:

- ⇒ Hit the snooze button at least once.
- ⇒ Spend at least 20 minutes or more on social media.
- ⇒ Start reading and responding to emails.

⇒ Consume a quick and unhealthy breakfast filled with carbs and sugar.
⇒ Spend at least 15 minutes trying to figure out what you're going to wear.

Now you know what I mean by morning rituals, and if yours have succeeded in making you unproductive, then it's time to change it.

Morning rituals set the tone for the entire day. Some of the most successful people in the world have daily rituals. According to Reggie Love, Former President Barack Obama's personal aide from 2009 to 2011, President Obama has a morning ritual. He starts every day with a 6:45 am workout, typically strength or cardio training, followed by green tea, orange juice or water. The late Steve Jobs, former Apple CEO, once said, "For the past 33 years I have looked in the mirror every morning and asked myself: 'If today were the last day of my life, would I want to do what I am about to do today?' And whenever the answer has been 'No' for too many days in a row, I know I need to change something."

Self-help guru Tony Robbins breaks morning rituals down into three increments, "15 minutes to fulfillment", "30 minutes to thrive" or an "hour of power". Tony himself starts his day with a plunge into an ice cold bath or pool. He once said he jumped into a river on a snowy day. Tony says he does this because it's the best way to awaken your system. Your morning routine doesn't have to be as radical as taking a dip into icy cold water or as simple as asking yourself a question in the mirror every morning, because as most things in life, morning rituals are not 'one size fits all'. As such, they would have to be tailored to suit your individual goals or needs. Engaging in these rituals are a great way of avoiding what social psychologist Roy F. Baumeister calls 'decision fatigue". We make thousands of decisions per day. We decide on everything from when we should wake up, what we should have for breakfast, whether we have time to stop at Starbucks for a coffee or if instead, we should go to Dunkin Donuts because it's closer to work. How many creams? How many sugars? You get my drift. When your brain is tired; the frontal cortex which is the part of the brain responsible for decision making, is less active. As a result of our brains being overly stimulated, we tend to 'zone out' and it is during this period when we're zoned out that we are prone to making the worst decisions ever. Baumeister is also quoted as saying, "Making decisions uses the very same willpower that you use to say no to doughnuts, drugs or illicit sex". He went on to say, "It's the same willpower that you use to be polite or to wait your turn or to drag yourself out of bed or to hold off going to the bathroom. Your ability to make the right investment or hiring decision may be reduced simply because you expended some of your willpower earlier when you held your tongue in response to someone's offensive remark or when you exerted yourself to get to the meeting on time." Practicing a morning ritual makes you less reactive, increases your productivity and conserves your decision making willpower. Decision fatigue is also the reason some people become minimalists. Have you ever noticed how some of the most successful people wear the exact same thing every day? Former American Idol judge Simon Cowell, Facebook Founder Mark Zuckerberg, and Fashion House Icon Karl Lagerfeld just to name a few. Although I'm sure they all have their personal reasons for doing so, it eliminates the decision of "what should I wear today". Perhaps you could benefit from having a decision free closet. Be honest with yourself; how long does it typically take you to find something to wear? It takes forever doesn't it? Not because you don't have any options but because you have too many options. Wouldn't it be simpler if you knew in advance exactly what you were going to wear? Reducing the amount of decisions you make daily actually frees up more mental space for smarter and more effective decisions. Although the minimalist lifestyle may not be for you, simplifying your life should be. Take a moment to write down what you can do at night before hitting the bed to ensure a less stressful morning. Make a habit of scheduling your days in advance. Then decide how long you are willing to devote to your morning ritual; 15 minutes, 30 minutes or an hour. Lastly, determine what your morning ritual will entail. Great examples of activities you could include in your ritual are:

- An ab or cardio workout
- Guided Meditation
- Yoga session
- Morning Walk or Run
- Writing in your gratitude Journal
- Prayer
- Quiet time in nature
- Drink A Glass of Lemon Water, Green Tea or Smoothie
- Take a multivitamin
- Recite your daily mantra or affirmations
- Daily Devotion or Scripture Reading
- Inspirational Podcasts
- Listen To Audiobooks
- Write today's intention in your daily planner

Rituals and routines are especially helpful for mothers. Schedule daily activities like nap time, bedtime and bath time. Consider meal prepping to take the "what's for dinner" question completely off the table. Simplifying your daily routine declutters the mind which reduces anxiety, relieves stress and allows you to free up more mental space.

Incorporating one new habit a day can change your entire life. I've recently adopted a new practice into my morning ritual. It's called morning pages. I was inspired by Julia Cameron's book, "The Artist's Way". The basic premise behind morning pages is to write 3 full pages of whatever is in your heart or mind. Write until the pages are full. Trust me, it sounds much easier said than done but when you do it, something truly remarkable happens. Truths that may be consciously or subconsciously buried are unearthed. Your deepest worries, concerns, dreams, hopes, desires, and fears are brought to the forefront. This very simple activity helps to bring clarity, exposes limiting beliefs and forces you to confront your inner critic.

In chapter one, we discussed the importance of visualization. The life you visualize for yourself should work in concert to your daily ritual or routine. For example, if you visualize yourself being physically fit and twenty pounds lighter, your morning ritual should include eating a healthy breakfast, writing in your food journal, activating your step counter app or pedometer and exercising. In other words, the life you visualized for yourself will require congruent daily action to get there. You didn't get to where you are right now overnight and so, you can't expect the change to be overnight either. For you to get from where you are to where you want to be, it will require consistent effort and a willingness to change. Activist Angela Davis said it best, "I am no longer accepting the things I cannot change. I am changing the things I cannot accept…" Life is not happening to you, it's happening with you. You have the power to create the life you've always wanted to live. You are actually making a choice by not making a choice, by being laid back and allowing life to happen to you-you are choosing to accept whatever comes your way and that in itself is a choice. Why not make the better choice of consciously determining how your life turns out?

# CONCLUSION

When a boxer is being trained he holds his hands up while being punched in his sides repeatedly. This process is called conditioning. It helps the fighter build up his endurance and increases his ability to withstand the pain of being hit. You are in the middle of the ring of life and life has been hitting you in your sides for years. You've been knocked down before but you've never been knocked out or you wouldn't be here. You have been training for this all your life and you are ready. Stop getting ready to get ready. Now is the time, now is your time! In the words of Rocky Balboa, "it's not the amount of times you get hit it's about how many times you can keep getting hit and keep moving forward." If this book does nothing else I hope that it helps you to realize that there has never been a more perfect moment for you to go after your dreams than now!

Made in the USA
Middletown, DE
20 June 2020